I CHOOSE TO HEAL

SHYTAZHIA PATTERSON, OLIVIA PONTOO, ANDREA MOOREHEAD, ABRIYA GRANT AND ALEXIS ROBINSON

No part of this publication may be reproduced, distributed, or transmitted in any form or by any means, including photocopying, recording, or other electronic or mechanical methods, without the prior written permission of the publisher, except in the case of brief quotations embodied in critical reviews and certain other noncommercial uses permitted by copyright law.

Unless otherwise noted, all Scripture quotations are from the King James Version of the Bible.
Copyright © 2000 Holman Bible Publishers. All rights reserved. Used by permission.

Copyright © 2024 by Sandra Coleman et al
All rights reserved.
ISBN: 9798884456532

Acknowledgements

We would like to thank God for this opportunity to share our story in such a vivid and candid manner. We want to dedicate this book to our families and friends for believing in us.

Foreward

Healing can be messy, but it is doable. Healing comes from having to face the agonizing pain that we all have had to endure and finally decided that we are not going to continue this journey of being a leper but making a choice to heal. This journey came about in 2018 when I got married for the third time(yes I said third) and with that I thought all of my trouble and pain would cease. God dropped this conference I Choose To Heal in my spirit and when it came to fruition, I thought I had mastered the healing process and had become successful in my journey. Can I tell you I didn't. After that conference, it seemed like for years my life was cast into what looked like a downward spiral and all the hurt, pain, disappointment, lies I heard and told myself began to come up on the scene like hot lava from a volcano. To add injury to insult, church and family life began to look sketchy as well. Fast forward, in 2021- 2023 major shifts started coming down the pipe like flies on dung(such a nice way of putting it). Everything that could possibly go wrong went wrong....or did it go right? I found myself feeling the lowest of the low but let me tell you once I came out of my "feelings" and asked God to reveal what He was doing in the midst of the pain I was experiencing and this is what He said to me, "You're not as broken as you think you are." I got up from that floor and gathered myself and decided to choose. The Holy Spirit reminded me that I have a choice and there is power in my choice; thus the birth of this powerful book.

When God laid on my heart to make 'I Choose To Heal' a book, the thought of it began to evolve into something unimaginable. After praying, the Lord laid a few women on my heart to help co-author this book and these are some of the women and their stories you will read. These women have labored and have been vulnerable enough to share their powerful story of their struggles, trauma, toxic relationships, etc and most importantly their triumphant journey to healing!

Healing is a virtue and it takes patience, grace and determination to see yourself on the other side of this so you can become a better version of yourself. Let's journey together and CHOOSE to heal!

With Love,
Sandra Coleman

Introduction

I
choose
to
heal
I choose to become the me that scares me
That woman
who radiates like new chrome rims
Fresh out of the hand wash car detail
I choose
 to live a life full of abundance
FULL
of prosperity
Knowing that there is nothing
No
There is NO thing
That can ever
Put an end
To the plan
 that YOU God made for me
Except for me
I choose to acknowledge
that im not just good enough,
 but Ive BEEN enough,

Ive always been IT
Ive always had IT
But I learned in this life
Some will still treat you like
SUGAR
HONEY
ICED
TEA
Ive always measured UP
To the standards of being
The only thing that ive grown to love to be
And baby that me
Unapologetically
Sun kissed brown skin,
Magically defined melanin
ive always been enough
Not fitting the normal fit of an IG model
But yet
There is no doubt
That when God made me
When He fearfully and wonderfully made ME
He took the very best of the Earth
And engrained them in my skin
I carry the wind of God in my stride
The fire of heaven in my eyes
I choose to walk with my head up high
and shoulders back
Because Im built like that

To Bounce back
Knowing
that it is God who has called me
Out of the darkness
And Into His marvelous Light
THIS light
That radiates
THIS light
That permeates
THIS light
That gravitates
And causes the very galaxy to orb around its existence
Because before it existed in me
There was HE
And after He won me over
HE became WE
Which is He and I
Me and Him
And We have been rocking every since
He gave me light
And He gave me life
Which can only be given and provided
Out of the love
Of my Savior
I choose to heal
Lady J
Jimmica Iston

Table of Contents

FROM TRAUMA TO TRIUMPH 2

BOTTLED TEARS: A MOTHER'S PRAYER .. 21

FROM PAIN TO PURPOSE, FROM MISERY TO MINISTRY 29

THE THREADS OF HEALING: UNVEILING STRENGTH 52

THE WAKE-UP CALL 74

CHAPTER 1 FROM TRAUMA TO TRIUMPH SHYTAZHIA'S STORY

At forty years old and married with children, I did not realize how much was bottled inside of me. I thought maybe I needed to deal with one specific area or two, but unfortunately, I had been suppressing brokenness for many years. I thought that I moved past the traumas, hurt, and disappointments until what was suppressed began to ooze out and hit the surface. The things that I was not free from were getting the best of me and I had to make a conscious choice to give it all to God and leave it there. I refused to let the issues of my past keep me hostage to the point that it affects my future.

As I was preparing myself for the I Am Free conference hosted by Sandra Coleman Ministries, I began to feel overwhelmed. I felt like life had me backed up against the ropes and was beating every bit of strength out of me. I looked in the mirror with tears and I told God, "I don't know how to do this". " I don't know how to be the strong person that You want me to be to carry the load". I cried and cried my heart out to God because I-WAS-JUST-TIRED. I asked the Lord to show me how to be the person He created me to be because I couldn't do it on my own. I had to pull myself together with the little strength I had and prepare for the conference.

Later that evening at the conference I felt the spirit of God pulling and tugging onto my spirit through the guest infuser. The things that I went to God about earlier that day were being reiterated and the same questions that I asked God about were being answered. I sat in my seat fighting back the tears because every single word that came forth was hitting me down to my soul. Moreover, when it was time for the altar call, I felt compelled to go because I knew God was already dealing with me. Once I got to the altar, the minister asked "Are you ready to be free?" As if she knew the message was for me. My response was " I got to be free". The minister began to pray over me and slowly, I felt myself lowering down to the floor. I cried out to God, telling Him I was tired and I wanted to be free from everything. The way that I cried, you would've thought someone had just died. As soon as I felt all cried out, I made my way off the floor, wiped my face, and headed back to my seat. Then, I was told to wait and stay where I was. The next thing I knew, every woman who was a spiritual leader encircled me to fight on my behalf. Furthermore, I started going through my deliverance process and I can remember the pain of the cry and the unusual sounds that were coming from within. I could hear what was going on from both realms; the physical and the spiritual. I was hearing the prayers that went forth and at the same time, I was hearing in the spirit. Suddenly, the traumatic experiences from my past began flashing before my eyes. Journey with me as I explain.

Memories

When I was a little girl, about the age of four or five, I remember spending a lot of time with my paternal grandparents. They used to come and pick me up from my mother's house just about every weekend, and sometimes I would stay the whole week with them. I used to be with my grandparents so much that I had a room at their house. Nobody couldn't tell me anything, I knew that I was my grandparent's baby.

With being with them and to my recollection, there was hardly ever one there without the other. Most of the time they worked together as a team when it came to me. I remember both of them teaching me how to ride my bike, playing hide and seek, and even playing with my cabbage patch dolls with me. When a task or activity only required one of them, the other was still around. For instance, when my grandmother used to wash and press my hair, my grandfather was right there, at the kitchen table playing solitaire. Whenever she cooked we sat at the kitchen table doing stuff together.

I have so many memories with my grandparents, including taking long bus rides that seemed like forever. Before it was time for us to get on the charter bus, my grandparents would prepare snacks, drinks, and even a light blanket for the ride. As we traveled, we went from a city view to a mountain view where trees were set off in the distance. I always loved getting on the road because I just loved to travel and go places. The thing that I did not fully understand about riding so far was the fact that we were going to see my father.

The place that we were going to on those long bus rides was a correctional institution where my father resided. He became incarcerated when I was two years old and was sentenced to serve twenty-five years to life for murder. Back then I did not understand what was going on. I didn't know any better than to think it was a normal thing and that's how life was supposed to be. I did not question anything about his absence at the time because I felt like I had everything I needed. My grandparents compensated as much as they could to make sure that I didn't lack anything. They were the bridge between us by providing and taking time with me as well as making sure that I saw him regularly to make sure he was a part of my life.

Unfortunately, things begin to change for me. I remember waking up one morning without the smell of food cooking in the kitchen. Therefore, I ran to the kitchen to see what was going on. My grandfather was sitting at the table with his black phonebook in his hand with a look on his face that I had never seen before. So I asked, "Where's grandma?". He didn't respond in any way as if he was stunned. I turned around and ran down the hall to their room to look for her and there she was lying in the bed. I walked over to her side of the bed and began to shake her "Grandma get up, grandma get up". Repeatedly, I called and shook her but there was no response. I figured she was still asleep but I noticed she was sweating profusely. Being that I didn't know any better, I went to get a towel to wipe her face but also noticed a funny stench coming from her as I wiped her face. I remember saying "Grandma time to get up and wash" but there was still no response. My grandfather made his way to the back to come get me to take me to the front. After some time, there was a knock on the door. I noticed there were men in gray and black uniforms coming into the house with a stretcher. I tried to look and see where they were going but my grandfather told me to stay with him. They went to the back and came back with a black bag zipped up. My grandfather had me on his lap in a tight hug, I guess so that I wouldn't move but as I looked at his face he appeared to be weeping softly. After the men made it out the door I ran to the back of the house to find that my grandmother was no longer there. I asked "Where is grandma?" and my grandfather broke down at the table.

Moreover, three years passed and I have seen my father less and less. My grandfather kept taking me to see my father as much as he could but he began having health complications. He was in and out of the hospital therefore, my father's oldest brother and sister came home to take care of him. They picked me up after school about three times a week to see my grandfather because he was sick, sadly he passed away a few weeks later. I was able to see my father at his funeral and that was the end of the visits. Nobody was willing to take me to see him after both of my grandparents passed away. From that point, my relationship with my father was through letters, cards, and telephone calls but as more time went by it became inconsistent. Distance came in between me and the man that I was getting to know as my father.

Shattered Innocence

As life continued without my grandparents, things seemed a little weird because it was something I was not used to. I know being with my grandparents helped my mother some because she always had to work. At home with my mother, there was always a house full of people. The house we stayed in was a multifamily home with three separate apartments that my mother and siblings resided in. I was satisfied that I had my brothers to play with as well as my cousins. When the majority of the adults went to work, and when we didn't have school, we were left with Uncle Shawn or Uncle Lance. Shawn was my mother's baby brother and Lance was just a family friend that they grew up with and called their brother.

Furthermore, I remember Uncle Shawn sleeping most of the time when he watched us because he was just a night owl, he slept all day and was up all night. I remember doing crazy things while Uncle Shawn was asleep, trying to be responsible and cook dinner for my mother before she came home from work. Undeniably, I was trying to cook by putting a bag of chicken in a large plastic storage bowl and into the oven. It's funny thinking about it because I thought I knew what I was doing when I didn't know what I was doing at all. I remember blaming it on Uncle Shawn and laughing to myself because I got away with it as if he didn't know any better. I have nothing but smiles when I think about Shawn watching us but on the other hand, my memory of Lance is dark and creepy.

There were times when there was no difference between Lance and the rest of my uncles, but there were times when there was a distinct difference. The difference was that Lance allowed the spirit of perversion to use him. One day, the adults went to work and all the children were left with Lance. We played from upstairs in my mother's apartment to downstairs in my aunt's apartment and headed out the back door to play hide and seek in the garage. As everyone was running around and hiding, Lance called me back into the house as if he needed me to do something. When I went back into the house, he pulled me to him and said "You are becoming a big girl, and big girls know how to keep secrets". He then continued and said "I want to show you something but you can't say anything ok?" Because I didn't know exactly what to do at that moment, I went along with what he said because I trusted him, and there in the back of the house, I was sexually abused. I was robbed of my innocence while an opening was presented for different spirits to attach themselves to me.

I didn't say anything as he instructed me not to, but one day something or someone made my mother suspicious about it. One evening when she came home, she called me into the room and felt the need to check my private area. Thankfully, she started paying more attention without me having to say anything because it never happened again after that. I don't remember what happened but I know Lance never put his hands on me again. For twenty years, I never told a soul about what happened to me until I had my own child. I finally said something about it upon getting off from work one afternoon. It was unfortunate that I received a phone call from my cousin Eesha asking if Lance had ever inappropriately touched me when we were children. My response to her was a hesitant "Yes". I asked Eesha "Where did that come from, and why are you asking me that?" I wondered how that came up after so many years, and to my surprise, she said "Me too". Eesha also mentioned that my sister and one other cousin said that it happened to them as well. My heart dropped in my stomach because I just felt like something had happened when she called me with the questions. Again, I asked, "How did that come up in conversation?" By her tone I knew she was livid. Eesha said, " I had seen the boys being kind of fresh; I asked them where they got that from and who taught them that?" She proceeded to say that our sons, who were four years old at the time, told her that they were fresh from Lance. I cut her off abruptly, "Hold up, what happened now?" Everything that I felt as a child came rushing back. I just told her, "I am on my way" and I hung up the phone. Moreover, when I pulled up to the house everyone was furious. The whole house was in an uproar. I felt the same way but after seeing how everyone was going crazy, I buried my feelings back down again because the feeling of discomfort and shame came over me again. I just remained quiet and observed everyone else's reactions. My family wanted to kill Lance that day but they spared him and put him out of the house. Our boys were fine and we just hadn't mentioned anything about that situation any more.

After all that time, I thought that I was fine. I suppressed so much that I forgot about it. As I searched for myself, I felt angry. I was angry with myself because I left my child vulnerable around a predator. I thought the sexual abuse ceased because it stopped with me plus the fact that nobody mentioned anything about it and it went on for years. Lance got away with committing the same act with all of the girls in the house because nobody said anything. I don't know what that spirit was sent to do within our household but I know it was an opening to something else.

Attachments

Becoming a woman I knew that there was something different about me because I had such a desire to have a different life from what I saw growing up. I did not want to just have kids but to have a complete family where a husband and father is present. That was something that was lacking in my home as a child. My father was not present due to his dealings in the streets and after I realized that some of my issues were rooted around him, I then became angry and resentful. The spirit of fear, rejection and abandonment had held me.

I was angry because of the things that happened in my life. I felt like my father was the one who was supposed to make sure his baby girl was safe at all times. I felt like he was supposed to be the first man in my life to set the standard, to set the tone for the next man that came after him. Additionally, I then looked at my mother in question, wondering why she never had those talks with me and helped me understand how I ought to be as a woman.

I kept looking for love, looking for my father in every relationship and falling in love with the thought of being in love. I went into each relationship without any standards and a lack of understanding the value that I held. I never saw myself the way God saw me and I dealt with a lot of degrading things in relationships. I was sexually abused as a child and when I got of age I was physically and emotionally abused. I was pistol whipped and beaten with a clothes iron. I was dragged by my leg out of the house while pregnant. I was told that no one else will want me or my kids. I also was told that if I lost weight I'd be more desirable. There's so much that I put up with in relationships and I promised myself that I would never allow myself to settle that low again.

Golden Nuggets

First, I want you to understand that it's imperative to personally know God before getting into any relationship. Developing an intimate relationship with Him will teach you how to love yourself the way that He loves you and setting the bar high enough that if a person wants you bad enough they will have to pursue you through God. Your personal relationship with God will build and reveal your true identity in Him.

Secondly, I suggest before investing time in a relationship, consult with God and wait for Him to show you if the person is right for you. Majority of the time people will connect and agree with covenants without consulting God and then we end up in a mess because that person may not be the person that compliments your purpose and where God is trying to take you. They can be a sent distraction to derail you. I did not have anyone to teach me these things before I started dating me. I learned as I went through and it was painful. My grandmother is a God fearing woman that taught me about Jesus and how to pray but conversations about relationships and being an honorable woman didn't happen. So If I can save someone from making the same mistakes and heartaches by sharing my experiences, I am here for it.

Lastly, date with a purpose. Don't be afraid to ask questions even if God gave the okay on the relationship. Always pray and keep God included in your relationship. One thing for sure and two things are for certain, is the fact that Satan hates union. Especially if there is purpose in it. Keep one another covered in prayer not just as your fellow mate or companion but as your brother or sister in Christ. We all fall short sometimes and the enemy is always watching and waiting so it's important to lift one another, encourage and speak life into one another. With Christ, the devil can't do nothing but be mad and take a back seat.

Final Thoughts

I began to have an understanding that everything that I faced was not to destroy me. I started to understand that God allows certain things to happen in our lives because He knows it will lead us right back to Him.

The more I grow in God, I can see the evidence of how I am growing. My knowledge of who Jesus is, has opened my understanding of who I am and who He has created me to be. Loving myself wasn't always easy because situations made me not realize my very own self worth but the moment I fell in love with Jesus, loving me became inevitable. I have come to the realization that holding on to past hurt and/or traumas can rob us of the peace and joy that Christ wants us to have. So I forgave my father for the mistakes he made as well as my mother because they did the best they knew how and couldn't give me something that they didn't have themselves. Therefore, if you have a parent that is or has been absent from your life, instead of being angry or resentful, allow the love of God that's within you to extend grace to them.

Moreover, we all have to revisit and face the pains from our past at some point and go through some type of deliverance. As long as we are living we will need to be delivered from something and it takes the power of God to give us strength and the understanding behind it so that the door can remain closed in order to keep moving forward. It takes effort to change and there has to be a conscious decision everyday to not turn back to your old ways. Freedom is a choice and if we desire to be free, our heavenly Father will not withhold that from us. It's easy to suppress, it's easy to smile and act like we are ok when deep down we can be dying inside. I know because I've been there. There is a root to every issue and the only way to conquer it is to face it head on, through Christ. His way not our way. Facing ourselves is vital, and no it will not feel good but it's necessary on the journey of healing. This is why I chose to heal and I am healing every day. There will always be triumph after trauma when you make a choice to heal. No matter how ugly or messy it looks, I challenge you to let go, give it all to God, and be free starting today. I challenge you to choose to heal!!

My Journal Notes

_____

_____

_____

_____

_____

_____

_____

_____

_____

_____

_____

_____

_____

_____

_____

_____

CHAPTER 2 BOTTLED TEARS: A MOTHER'S PRAYER

OLIVIA'S STORY

Loss is hard. In fact, it can be downright debilitating if you let it. In my case I've had many losses as in the physical death of people that I love. I've had losses through divorce, and I've even had the loss of a few friends or at least those who I thought were friends. But what I'm going through right now is the loss of someone near and dear to my heart who isn't gone physically, as in dead, but that has chosen to separate themselves from me emotionally and I've had to come to terms with the fact that they are in a place where they are not ready or able to release and forgive in order for there to be a renewal and restoration of our relationship.

My name is Olivia, but most people know me by Cookie. That's the nickname I've had all my life and it's not because I love to eat cookies-- which I NOW do-- but because my mom started calling me that as a baby before I could even eat cookies. I had asked her once where that nickname came from and she told me there used to be a girl on the soap opera that she liked named Cookie, so she started calling me that, but then she just chuckled to herself, so I never really knew if it was true or not. Either way it has stuck. My father was in the military so by the time I was 14 we had traveled 3 times overseas and to about 4 states in the U.S. My parents made sure to introduce me to the Christian faith and I don't remember wherever we were that we didn't go to church. I actually grew up believing that that's what every family does until I got a little older and realized that that just wasn't the case. However, it was a part of my upbringing and continued to be so even as I reached adulthood and eventually in my marriage and after having children of my own. Needless to say, while in the church I've seen a lot, heard a lot from the members of the congregation, workers in the church and from the ministers in the pulpit. My children were all born and raised in the church so it never occurred to me that they would one day decide the church was not where they wanted to be, but that's exactly what happened to me with three of my four children. It literally broke my heart. For a long time, I thought I had done something wrong, however, I had to realize that they each had to find their own way and that I could not push them into serving God. MY God. He had to become THEIR God and I had to lead by example and compel them to serve the God I serve and return to the church. So, after MUCH "wailing and gnashing of teeth", I took my hands off of it and I prayed. . . and prayed. . . and then prayed some more. Today, I'm happy to say that two of them have returned and one is still trying to find their way. However, through all of this, the one that did NOT leave the church hurt me the most while still IN the church. You know the enemy uses the very thing or things that we love the most to try and break us. I can honestly say that he almost succeeded. I mean how could my own child, the child I carried, the child I labored with for over 18 hours, who was raised in the church and taught to love, forgive, extend grace towards others, while being taught the principles of restoration and reconciliation ultimately tell me that they had not forgive me for leaving the church we served in together for over 25 years and for supposedly not supporting them in particular life decisions. So, once again I found myself wondering what I had done wrong.

I am literally in my 7th year of dealing with this situation and it's truly by the grace of God that I am still here with a sane mind loving God and loving God's people as I navigate through this process of healing. I guess you could say that I've been through what most people would call church hurt and many people don't understand how I do what I do with such grace--so I've been told. All I can say is, "BUT God"!

Have you ever had to love someone from a distance? Well, I have. I'm in the process of doing it now and honestly, I don't know if I'm doing it quite right because I don't know what "right" looks like. The question that I've often asked God is "why"? Why is this happening? Why is this happening to me? What did I do to deserve it? And of course, I have not come up with any answers or at least not anything that is satisfactory in my mind, but I do know this it's brought me to a place in God that I may not have reached

if I had not gone through-- and continue to go through -- had it not happened. It's definitely building my faith and making me TOTALLY dependent on HIM.

So how did I get here? Good question! I've had to ask myself that question over and over again. I've often heard it said freedom isn't free. It cost somebody something. It may not have cost you. It may not have cost me, but somebody paid a price. In order to get to my place of freedom --well I'm still a work in progress-- there have been many tears, many prayers, many questions --some with no answers-- but lots of faith and belief that God is going to do just what He said. I know that HE paid the price for MY freedom, and I just have to have faith that in the end "All things will work together for my good". It's been said --well actually it's in the Bible -- that God will have no other idols before Him. It's one of the 10 commandments. People will quickly say, "I'm not an idol worshiper. I'm not worshiping other gods". But if we're really honest about it, people—me included--unfortunately tend to put other people, places or things ahead of God and they hold a place in our hearts where only he should dwell. He is a jealous God, and he wants all of our worship to flow only to him. If I'm truly honest my children were my world and I put them on a pretty high pedestal. Maybe God was trying to get my attention. Maybe at that time, I focused too much on THEM and not enough on HIM. Well God knows how to get your attention and He has mine.

There's a scripture in the Bible that says after you've done everything you can, to stand. I have had no other choice BUT to stand; Stand on the word of God to believe that EVERYthing He promised He will do! So, I've come to Encourage you today. Things might be looking pretty bad. In fact, things are not going the way that you had planned at all. If it were up to you things would not be looking the way they are looking and you would definitely do it differently. You've come to your wits end and you want to throw in the towel. Yes, I've been there. But I've come to realize that we have everything to lose and nothing to gain if we try to do it our way. THAT hasn't worked for us yet! Now has it? So, my strategy has been to continue in His word, continue to pray, continue to believe in faith, visualize every day what it is that I am believing for and not to waver or be moved by what I see or how I feel. I'm determined for God to get the glory, even in THIS!

My Journal Notes

CHAPTER 3 FROM PAIN TO PURPOSE, FROM MISERY TO MINISTRY

ANDREA'S STORY

I have an important story to tell you that will not take long, so take a ride with me down memory lane. My prayer is that someone is healed, delivered, strengthened and most of all prepared for whatever life throws your way. Let us travel back to April of 2010, when I was a 22-year-old graduating Senior, majoring in Psychology at THE Paine College in Augusta, Ga. I was preparing to defend my senior research, graduation in May and starting Grad School in August. Life was very promising for me, and I had a bright future ahead.

My mother came down 2 weeks before graduation with my niece Taniya (Sweet Thang) from my hometown Detroit, MI and helped me prepare to defend my senior field but most importantly, graduation. She cleaned my townhouse from top to bottom, cooked me breakfast every morning, dinner every night, the luxury of having home cooked meals (which is every broke college student dream) and having my #1 cheerleader there meant the world to me. My mother was my first best friend, and we were extremely close. So, the day came, and it was time for me to defend my Senior Research! My mom and Sweet Thang cheered me on as I presented my research in the room with critiquing Professors and peers.

I was so nervous and all I could remember was seeing my mom's beautiful face, bright smile, and head nod assuring me, "You got this." I took a deep breath and I presented by far the best Senior Research (If I must say) that year and so on. My professors, peers, and most of all my mom were so proud. My mom gave me the biggest hug and we celebrated with dinner and created new memories. This was the highlight of my life! God had truly smiled on me.

In the next two weeks, the highly anticipated moment came as friends and family gathered around on May 2nd, 2010, to watch Andrea Nicole Moorehead receive her bachelor's of arts in Psychology. As I walked across the stage while my name was being called, I could literally hear my mom screaming at the top of her lungs while shedding tears of joy and jumping up and down like an immensely proud Mom. We took pictures and celebrated with our family, friends and my closest college friends to celebrate our achievements. This was one for the books.

After graduation, I was able to go home (Detroit) for the summer which was an extreme blessing because I had a part-time job at Payless. I was able to keep my job while away and really focus on celebrating and spending time with my family and friends. This summer will always be one to remember because my mom and I started having more intimate conversations and really started to become closer as she is accepting that I was no longer her baby but an educated and responsible adult. She expressed how much she disliked the guy I was dating (lol) as we laughed, cried and she clarified some things I did not understand regarding my family and between her and my dad. These intimate conversations, wisdom and clearer understanding I will always hold near and dear.

During the summer, we took family pictures with my mother's side of the family and almost everyone was there. My uncle who served in the Navy and was deployed for over 2 years came home and the family spent a lot of time together. I had a graduation party and God really allowed us to unite as a family and spend a lot of time together without commotion, bickering or pettiness which was a beautiful thing. Also, during the summer I received my schedule for Grad school which I was excited about and the first class I was scheduled to take was Grief Counseling. Never would I ever imagine this would be for my own destiny. Nevertheless, I was really waiting for the next chapter of my life to start.

As the summer ended, I returned to Augusta, GA to start Grad School at Troy University. I will never forget my first day in class. We did an assignment that consisted of identifying members of our family that would have the most impact on us if they died. As a supreme daddy's girl and him being the lead of the house, I choose him, not because I favored one parent over the other but simply for two reasons: I truly thought my mom would live longer and that my dad is such an amazing provider for us, and we are always protected and cared for without question. This assignment also gave us insight into how much funerals cost, the process of how they work and most importantly, the grief that comes along with it. This first week was very insightful, and I could not wait to speak with my mommy about what I was learning.

I remember calling her and she stated, "Yes, death is something else, no one wants to prepare for and extremely expensive. But guess what, we all must go and return to Father God." She also jokingly asked me when I was getting my refund check and that she was so proud of me. We hung up and we said I love you. After this conversation, as weeks went by, some people in our church and community died and my mom started sharing some dreams she was having and asked me, "Do you think God should start preparing people or show them signs before they die?" I answered, "I don't know Ma Dux, what do you think?" She answered, "Yes, most definitely. Especially when you are connected to Him." I did not think anything of it because it was not out of the norm for my mom to attend EVERYBODY funeral, she always talked about death and prepared me for what would happen whenever she passed away and she always expressed how she was not afraid to die because she knows Jesus for herself, worships and praises him. A true spiritually gifted woman of God.

As the months passed, this was in September of 2010 and school was going well and so far, I was maintaining an A in the class. I got a phone call from my little sister that my oldest niece called 911 because my mom was in severe pain and passed out. My mom developed 6 kidney stones and 3 were small enough to pass on their own and a stint was needed for the other 3 to pass. She had a small operation to insert the stint. The procedure was successful, and she recovered well. Over the next month, I spoke with her, and she seemed to be in great spirits. I continued attending classes every week, my relationship dissolved, and I wanted to go out and have a nice dinner by myself. I remember calling my mom after class and she sounded out of it. She was in the hospital to get her stint removed because the other 3 kidney stones passed through successfully. I told her I loved her and to get some rest, little did I know that our last conversation would be the last.

After the conversation with my mom, I went over to a friend's house and hung out there. I was so tired from that day, I fell asleep on the couch, and my phone was on vibrate so I did not hear it ringing. It was about 8am the next morning and my friend woke me up saying, "your phone is ringing." When I looked at my phone, I had about 30 missed calls and my cousin was calling again. When I answered the phone I said, "What's wrong with my momma?" She said, "You talked to your dad?" I said, "No, I can just feel something is wrong with my mom, especially since no missed calls are from her." My cousin paused, took a deep breath, and said, "you are right cuz, it is your mom. She had a massive stroke, and you need to get home ASAP." I grabbed my keys immediately and headed home.

On my drive home, I started praying and asking God for instant miracles and that His angels would protect and comfort my mom and family. I learned the voice of God at an early age, was spiritually gifted and wise at an early age and during undergrad, everyone knew that I loved God and that I was a "Jesus Freak." I would blast my gospel mixtapes around campus, host bible studies at my house and everyone knew where to come if they needed any guidance, prayer or just a listening ear. I didn't club, drink, curse, have sex and do anything that was unpleasant to God. I read my bible, attended church regularly, danced at church, tithed and committed myself to being a willing vessel for God, to say the least, I walked righteously and took pride in being a TRUE follower of Christ. So, I knew that God would hear my prayers and heal my mom because I was "on fire" for him.

As I packed and headed to the airport, I continually prayed and listened to gospel music on my phone. I was anxious and nervous because I had to fly standby, and all the flights were booked so it took a couple of hours for me to get to Detroit. Nevertheless, I was patient and I finally got on the plane and made it to Detroit that evening. I remember getting to the car and seeing the distress look on my dad's face. I knew this was not looking good. He was silent and had extraordinarily little to say. When we got to the hospital he said, "shorty imma be honest with you, it's not looking good, and your mom is in bad shape."

I remember telling him, "It's ok Pops, I can handle it." So, as we walked into the hospital and got on the elevator, I remember taking some deep breaths and preparing myself for whatever I was about to see. As I entered the room, my mom's body was out of whack, and they could not calm her down enough to insert an IV. I remember leaning in and whispering in her ear, "hey girl, I'm here." Her body instantly relaxed and calmed down, and they inserted the IV. It was as if she was waiting for me to get there. I prayed over her, gave her a forehead kiss, and proceeded to go to the waiting room where my family was. Somehow, there was a peace and a sense of strength that came over me.

In the waiting room, my family looked defeated and worried. I wanted to brighten up the mood and instill some faith, so I hugged everyone, and we prayed as a unit. We arranged shifts that everyone would take so that my mom was never left alone, especially if any medical decisions needed to be made. The next day, we all arrived at the hospital; word was out that my mom had had a stroke, so church members, her friends and more family members began coming to visit her. I took everyone into the chapel, and I led prayer and made it my business to set the tone for what was expected before they entered the room. I instructed everyone that they had to enter the room with great spirits, no crying, only prayers and scriptures were allowed during this time. Everyone who visited my mom was receptive to my wishes.

So as time passed that day, the doctor came out and told us that my mom was fighting for her life, she had a massive stroke, and that she would probably have to learn how to walk, talk, and do other motor skills again and that she would need to go to rehab after they discharged her from the hospital. We remained hopeful and continued to make sure we were on our assigned shifts. The next day, during an examination, a doctor noticed that my mom's left foot felt cold, and it was a major concern and that he wanted to operate and figure out what was causing the lack of or no circulation in her leg. They gave us the rundown of the medical state my mom was in and how risky it was to operate but it was necessary. We agreed and prayed, and the surgery was a success.

After surgery, the doctors stated that my mom needed a trachea to help with her breathing and we gave consent to do so. My mom had been through so much in such an abbreviated time span, it was less than a week. As she continued to recover, we were at the hospital nonstop, and we continued taking shifts and being by my mom's side. She would open her eyes often, but the doctor's stated that when a patient is in a sedated coma, the nerves in their brain will make their eyes open from time to time. As a family of faith and followers of Christ, we knew better.

The doctors also stated that her kidneys were not functioning properly and that she may need to be on dialysis. We informed the doctor to give it sometime and allow her to rest before we made any more drastic decisions since she had already been through so much. We prayed about it, and her kidneys started functioning again. We serve a prayer answering God that is faithful and true to every promise and word that He has spoken and written.

We understood that the bible says in 1 Thessalonians 5:16-17: "Rejoice always, pray without ceasing, give thanks in all circumstances..." "Rejoice always, pray without ceasing, give thanks in all circumstances; for this is the will of God in Christ Jesus for you." We also knew that Isaiah 53:5 (KJV); But he was wounded for our transgressions, he was bruised for our iniquities: the chastisement of our peace was upon him; and with his stripes we are healed. Most importantly, Philippians 4:13 (KJV); "I can do all things through Christ which strengtheneth me." We knew that God was working on her behalf and giving us comfort and strength in this process.

A month had passed, and everything the doctors had concerns about became miracles. They stated that she wasn't responding to their voice but she would respond to ours. My aunt told us that my mom watched an episode of family feud with her and my big sister said that she asked my mom questions and she would respond (without speaking of course). My mom was very stubborn so we would jokingly say, "she doesn't know the doctor's so of course she's not going to respond to you."

My mom started showing signs of improvement and the next step towards her recovery was rehab. We were excited to get her out of the hospital with hopes that she would come home soon. I was constantly going back and forth from Augusta to Detroit because I still had to attend my grad school classes. Surprisingly, I was still acing my classes with all A's and the second class I took was substance abuse. I would call my family and get frequent updates on my mom, even though I wanted to be by her side. However, they were adamant about me staying in school.

When I arrived back in Detroit, it was November and almost Thanksgiving. My mom was still in rehab, however this day was very significant. They were trying to wean her off the breathing machine and slowly take her out of sedation but everytime they started the process, her vitals would shoot up. That indicated that something was wrong. The next step was for her to see a neurologist.

The appointment wasn't right away so we continued to visit her at rehab and most importantly, pray for a speedy recovery. I continued going back and forth and came home when I could. My professors were aware of everything and continued to show extreme grace during this season. I continued praying, attending church and believing God to heal my mom.

Well, December came and my mom's neurologist appointment came around. I remember it like it was yesterday. The neurologist told our family that my mom needed to have her brain scanned to see why her vitals kept elevating up whenever they tried to wean her off the breathing machine. The results would come back in a few days. Those days felt like months, however we were still praying for a miracle.

After we received the results, it was the most devastating news of my life. I remember my family calling me saying, "hey we're having a family meeting." Anytime I've heard that it was to discuss either something serious or a "lemon squeeze". Everyone was at the meeting in person, however I was in Augusta and on speakerphone. The meeting started and the only thing I really heard was, "Jenny's brain stem is damaged and she won't ever be able to breathe on her own. She'll always be in a vegetative state. We're all here to see how everyone is feeling and to make a decision on what the next step will be."

Everyone was stating how they felt, and came to a conclusion to take her off of the ventilator. Well, everyone but me. I did not agree with everyone's vote. "Andrea, Jenny is suffering." I also remember being angry with my Dad because he was so frustrated that I didn't want to face our reality. For God's sake this was my mother and my best friend we are talking about. I couldn't believe what I was facing.

I couldn't wrap my mind around voting for such a difficult decision but clearly I was out voted. I called my big sister and cried like a baby. I remember saying, "You're telling me that I could lose my mom. She won't see me graduate, get married or anything monumental in my life." She answered, "Unfortunately sis, this is what we're facing. We're leaving it up to God."

We decided on a date that would officially start this process of seeing If God would perform a miraculous miracle or if He would take her home. This date was December 19th and as the weeks passed, I remember praying for a miracle because at 22 years old, I couldn't imagine my life without my mother. I remember that day, I headed to Augusta airport (AGS) and I was so anxious and out of it. I ran into one of my college big brothers and he was also trying to get out of Augusta to fly somewhere as well.

We couldn't get out of Augusta because we both were flying standby, so he extended the offer for me to ride with him to Atlanta. He had no idea what I was facing because I'm naturally a bubbly and positive person. As we traveled to Atlanta, we talked and he asked me, "Where are you headed little sis?" I said, "I'm going back to Detroit for the holidays and take my Mom off of life support."

He couldn't believe what I just told him and he stated how strong I was and how he was praying for me and my family. We continued chatting and next thing we knew, we were at Atlanta airport (ATL). We hugged and went our separate ways and I was on my way to Detroit. While on the plane, I remember being in heavy worship, praying and asking God for strength.

I made it to Detroit and either that same day or the next day, we went to the hospital. My mom's Pastor came so we sang, prayed and waited. As the hospital staff (doctors and nurses) began to wean my mother off life support, she started to go into something like cardiac arrest. We had a no resuscitate order so if God would've taken her then, we would've had to deal with it.

However, God saw differently, and the hospital staff was able to give her a morphine drip (IV) and allow "nature" to take its course. I stayed in the room for 2 straight days watching my Mom and still believing God for a miracle. I also remember being in the room, watching my Mom go from breathing easily to struggling to breathe. It was now December 21st, and after a few hours something began to happen.

I was napping and all I heard was someone say, "Oh my God! Somebody find a nurse." My mom began to vomit everywhere and the nurses came to clean her up. After they finished, I checked to make sure she was still breathing and she was. Less than 20 minutes later, she began to vomit everywhere again, however this time when they flipped her over on one side she was still breathing. They then flipped her on the other side and she was still breathing, but after they placed her back center she took her last breath.

I looked at the nurse and asked her if she was gone, and she took her pulse and shook her head yes. I couldn't believe the woman who God chose to carry me, my first best friend and my everything was gone. I also couldn't believe I witnessed my mom die right before my eyes. My family was in complete shock, they cried, my baby sister screamed and we leaned on each other for strength. Me on the other hand, I couldn't cry, this was the first time I felt completely numb and out of my body and mind.

Christmas came and we had to break the news to my nieces and nephew about their Granny. They were devastated and knowing that they were hurting made us all hurt. My mother was their favorite person and they were hers. Christmas was my mom's favorite holiday and the holiday's would never be the same.

We started planning the funeral, and I was very vocal about who I wanted to prepare my mother's body. My family agreed and we started this process. That same night, I went to the "White bar" with my family and I got lit! All I could think of and see was my mom taking her last breath. I couldn't sleep at all and the only way I knew I would rest was if I was either tipsy or drunk. I remember the next day or so going to the funeral home and all I could ponder on was the promises I made to my mom when I was 16.

I promised I would be strong and that I would make sure I honored her wishes. I picked out her casket, designed her headstone, helped with her outfit and wig and wrote a beautiful passage in the obituary for me and my sisters. It appeared that I inherited my mother's strength when she passed away. I didn't shed a tear at the funeral and I even spoke and made everyone laugh. When I tell you my mother looked so beautiful, youthful and at peace, it gave me peace.

After the funeral and the rest of the holidays, it was finally time for me to return to Georgia. I was getting ready to start back school which was also divine alignment, Substance Abuse was my next class. I never understood why these classes were back to back but they were definitely for my good. I drank alcohol everyday and I didn't notice what was happening or what habit was forming. Alcoholism runs in my family and I never thought that I was becoming one.

During this course, one of the assignments was to go to either an AA or NA meeting or and write about your experience. Let's keep in mind that I'm not an alcoholic (so I thought) so I automatically choose NA (Narcotic Anonymous). At this NA meeting, it was so amazing watching people who were years, months, weeks and even days clean. It is such a spiritual experience and it made me understand that drugs are more of a disease than a struggle or addiction.

I completed my assignment and a few days later, my friend/classmate called me asking me if I would go to an AA meeting with her because she didn't want to go alone. She didn't know that I was struggling and what I was going through. She was aware that I lost my mom though. We went to the meeting and it was more amazing than the NA meeting. Going to AA is such a spiritual awakening and it is Christian based which made me feel like I was at home. Listening to people's testimonies and how they are "taking it one day at a time" was empowering.

At the end of the meeting, I had a divine revelation. I realized that I was becoming an alcoholic. I announced it to everyone and my friend was in shock. Before going to this, I was praying for God to restore my peaceful sleep but now I was more intentional about God taking the taste out of my mouth. The meeting ended and I realized that I had some serious work to do to heal and be restored.

I continued to pray for God to take the taste out of my mouth and baby, be careful about what you pray for! God answered that prayer immediately! There wasn't a time I drank something and didn't get sick. No matter how much I consumed (little or small), I always felt it and I started having my hangovers while I was drinking. The weirdest thing ever!

6 months passed and I was so angry with God, He took my baby away from me. I still hadn't fully grieved over the loss of my mom. I never cried and I didn't fully accept that she was gone. In my mind, she was on vacation, on a cruise and never coming back. That was

my way of coping until one night, I was sitting in my bed, my room was dark, a light flashed on the side of my right eye and I heard a voice. The voice said loud and clear, "She was never yours."

That tore me up and I began sobbing like a baby. It reminded me that our parents are loaners just like we're loaned to them. We all belong to God and we're only here for a little while until we complete our mission. From that day forward, my TRUE healing process started. I began operating in my misery and turning it into ministry. Today, I am proud to say that God has truly delivered me from alcohol, and I have no desire to drink it and I don't crave it anymore.

Today, I am proud to say 13 years later, that I have accomplished a lot of achievements and overcame any weapon or obstacle that has come my way. I continue to mentor and testify to others about how to navigate through this life after you have lost a parent. God continues to use me as a vessel for His Kingdom and I am honored He chose me to preach His living word. This road hasn't been easy by no means, but it's definitely been divine and worth it.

I've been able to help a lot of people along the way and produce a brand that also helps people via social media (YouTube, etc.) and it is also helping me along the way. Losing a parent is never easy but it's easier to bury them because it's way more difficult the other way around. I have witnessed it and it's a dreadful and painful thing to witness. The Bible says in Proverbs 22:6 (KJV) Train up a child in the way he should go: And when he is old, he will not depart from it. Without my mother's drive and obedience with the Lord's will over her life, I wouldn't be where I am today.

Losing her was the hardest thing I've experienced thus far. I have grown and changed so much. My attachment to people isn't the same because my umbilical cord has been literally cut. I've lost so many so-called friends, distanced myself from family, turned my back on God but one thing that has never changed and it is that God has remained constant and faithful even when I was angry and disobedient.

In closing, I want to encourage anyone that has gone through such a traumatic loss as myself and tell you that there is light at the end of the tunnel. Maybe you haven't experienced this yet, but one day you will. NEVER stop trusting God even when it's difficult and you're angry with how things have panned out. Temporary situations don't affect a permanent God! Remain faithful, prayerful and hold on to God's unchanging hands! I love you!

My Journal Notes

CHAPTER 4 THE THREADS OF HEALING: UNVEILING STRENGTH ABRIYA'S STORY

The Tangled Threads

The first chapter of my life was marked by threads of pain and adversity. As I navigated the complexities of my early years, I found myself entangled in the web of past traumas and societal expectations. The wounds I carried seemed insurmountable, casting shadows on my self-worth and dimming the light of my spirit. But little did I know, these very threads, woven from pain and strength, would eventually form the fabric of my resilience.

Growing up, the scars of my past experiences remained unseen. I was a young woman shaped by the wounds of abuse, betrayal, and a sense of not belonging. The weight of these experiences shaped the lens through which I viewed the world, leading me to question my value and worthiness of love. Societal and family expectations further complicated my journey. The pressure to conform to predefined roles and definitions of success only fueled my internal struggle. I yearned for validation and acceptance, seeking to prove my worth through accomplishments that I hoped would quell the doubts that lingered within me.

As time marched on, I began to recognize that the threads of my life were tangled and knotted. The pain I carried was a burden that I bore silently, shielding my family and the world from the depth of my wounds. The veneer of strength I presented masked the vulnerability and the fragility that laid beneath the surface.

But even so, a glimmer of light emerged. The mustard seed of hope was planted through the support of loved ones who were able to see beyond my facade and encouraged me to find my voice. The small whispers of strength began to grow, a butterfly effect; the event of small changes leading to significant outcomes overtime. A spirit within me that refused to be extinguished. Sarah Jakes Roberts, a motivational speaker, author, and pastor said once that "Your past is just a story. And once you realize this, it has no power over you".

The tangle of threads that defined my early years was not a permanent state, but rather a challenge to be unraveled. The journey ahead promised healing, growth, embracing vulnerability, and ultimately, finding the freedom to rewrite my own story.

The Journey Within

This chapter of my life is about delving into the depths of my soul, facing my demons, and emerging with newfound clarity. The turning point arrived when I faced the most challenging chapter yet. In 2020, tragedy struck me when I lost my beloved grandfather to a sudden and shocking incident of strangulation days prior to my upcoming birthday. The pain of this loss was deep and profound, and it tested my faith and emotional fortitude.

Despite the devastation, I found the courage to lean on my support system, my faith, and the coping mechanisms I had developed over the years. Just when I was beginning to cope with the loss of my grandfather, the world was plunged into the grip of the COVID-19 pandemic in 2021. In rapid succession, I lost three more family members to the virus and its complications. The weight of grief was almost unbearable, and I felt as though my foundation had been shattered. The pandemic restrictions made it difficult to gather and mourn, adding an extra layer of stress and pain to my already overwhelming loss. There is never a day that does not go by when I wish there was a sliver of a chance to speak to each of them one last time. After months of depression and increased anxiety, I sought therapy for myself. I then realized that healing required confronting these wounds with courage and compassion. Through therapy, I learned to navigate the complex emotions of grief, to honor my feelings without judgment, and to gradually find a way forward. It was a process that demanded vulnerability—an admission of pain, loss, and the moments that had shaped me. The losses brought me face to face with the fragility of life. I felt anger, sadness, and an overwhelming sense of unfairness. At times, I questioned my faith and my ability to find meaning in the midst of such a profound tragedy. Through introspection and guided reflection, I began to discern the patterns that held me captive for so long. The more I acknowledged my pain and embraced my experiences, the more I discovered the outpour of strength that had always been within me.

Every journey within is not without its challenges. There were moments when I stumbled upon memories that were difficult to revisit, wounds that still carried the weight of the initial impact. But with each step forward, I was releasing myself of each heavy chain that bound me over the years. Therapy also provided a safe space for me to address my fears and anxieties about parenting my child amidst each loss. I worried about being emotionally available for my child while dealing with my own grief. The therapist helped me explore these concerns and develop strategies to create a nurturing environment while also taking care of my own mental well-being. I was and still is committed to healing and becoming the best version for myself and for my child. Still I incorporate these learnings daily, setting aside dedicated time for reflection and self-care. I engaged more in volunteer activities that brought me joy and a sense of purpose. As I navigated the twists and turns of my continued journey within, I hope to continue to be an advocate for mental health awareness, breaking the stigma surrounding seeking professional help. No longer feeling trapped in societal expectations; I choose to depthin my self-awareness and align my actions with God. The journey within is far from over, but I already embarked on a path that would lead me to a place of love, strength, and purpose. My prayers are more than just words but a powerful navigational tool that helps me continue to stay in alignment for what I asked God to do in my life.

A Nurturing Love

As I continued on my journey of healing and growth, I faced a new challenge within my personal life. My relationship with the father of my child began to unravel, revealing deep-seated issues that had been hidden beneath the surface. The lack of emotional support, understanding, and recognition of my progress became increasingly apparent. I found myself feeling isolated and hurt, especially as I put in the effort to heal and create a better life for myself and my child.

The pivotal moment came just four days before my birthday, when the father of my child suggested that they should simply be friends while they were still living together. This abrupt revelation was a blow to my heart, leaving me feeling betrayed and rejected. While the relationship had been strained for some time, the timing and manner of his announcement did not heightened the emotional turmoil I was already experiencing. I was at ease to know that my heart was in the healing process.

Amidst the weight of grief, my ongoing mental health journey, and now the strain in my relationship, I faced a crossroads during my graduate program. I was faced with the choice of whether to allow this setback to define me or to use it as an opportunity for further growth and self-discovery. Drawing from my wellspring of resilience, I chose the latter.

With the support of my therapist, friends, and community, I confronted my feelings of heartbreak and rejection head-on. I allowed myself to grieve the loss of the relationship, acknowledging the pain it brought while also reminding myself of my worth and the progress I had made. I learned to set healthy boundaries and communicate my needs, advocating for myself in ways I hadn't before.

My focus shifted toward creating a stable and nurturing environment for my child amidst the changes. I decided to prioritize co-parenting and open communication with the father of my child, seeking to ensure that our child's well-being remained the central concern. While the romantic relationship had ended, I recognized the importance of maintaining a healthy dynamic for the sake of our child's happiness and stability.

Often, I found myself reminding myself of the role I was now in—one that shaped the trajectory of my life in ways I couldn't have imagined. Motherhood is both a challenge and a gift, a canvas on which I could paint a narrative of unconditional love, growth, and authenticity.

The moment I held my child in my arms, I was struck by the weight of responsibility and the boundless reservoir of love that had awakened within me. It was a love that defied the scars of my past, a love that saw beyond the wounds I carried, and a love that yearned to provide the stability and nurturing that had once eluded me.

Nurturing love was not just about caring for my child's physical needs; it was about creating a safe space where vulnerability could thrive and authentic connections could flourish. In a world that often encouraged masks and pretense, I vowed to create an environment where my child felt seen, heard, and valued for who they truly were.

With each lullaby I sang, each story I read, and each moment of laughter we shared, I was rewriting the narrative of love that had been handed down to me. I discovered that nurturing love was as much about listening as it was about speaking—a practice that required me to attune myself to my child's needs and emotions.

But nurturing love wasn't limited to my role as a mother. It extended to the relationships that surrounded me—the bonds with family, friends, and mentors who had supported me on my journey. These connections were woven into the fabric of my healing, reminding me that I was not alone and that my journey was intertwined with the journeys of others.

One of the most crucial lessons I learned in this chapter was the importance of self-love. Nurturing love began with extending the same compassion, patience, and understanding to myself that I offered to my child. I recognized that my journey of growth was ongoing, and that moments of stumbling and imperfection were part of the process. Just as I nurtured my child's growth, I nurtured my own—forgiving myself for past mistakes and embracing the potential for future growth even with a failed relationship.

I was balancing being a single parent and a graduate student. This was very demanding, to say the least. My days were filled with parenting responsibilities, juggling coursework, and self care. The nights often found me burning the midnight oil to complete assignments while my child slept peacefully. My classmates and professors became a source of inspiration, reminding me I was not alone in this. I continued to make it a priority to carve out moments for quality with my child. These shared experiences are cherishable memories that I hold dear and my commitment to finishing my MBA program remained steadfast. As I continue on my journey of perseverance and healing, I faced a new challenge with my personal life.

Through this experience, I had a deeper understanding of what it meant to love and respect myself. I realized that my worth wasn't determined by the validation or recognition of others, but by the strength of my character, my commitment to growth, and my ability to navigate challenges with grace and resilience. I hope one day to share my stories with my child—the triumphs and the trials, the moments of joy and the moments of pain. In doing so, teaching them that authenticity was a strength, and that acknowledging our vulnerabilities was a step toward building deeper connections.

As the pages of chapter 3 turned, It taught me that love was a force of transformation—a force that could heal wounds, rewrite narratives, and inspire us to become the best versions of ourselves. Through nurturing love, I discovered the potential for growth, the beauty of vulnerability, and the capacity of the human heart to create a world that was rooted in authenticity, connection, and boundless love. Unexpected Beginnings

Months after the separation from the father of my child, I found I was at a crossroads of healing and new beginnings. The decision to go on a cruise in July, celebrating my long-time friend's upcoming wedding, was a way for me to embrace a new chapter in my life. The break from routine of parenting and coursework allowed me to recharge, connect with friends, and reflect on the journey I had undertaken.

As the cruise sailed into August, my path took an unexpected turn. It was at my friend's wedding that I encountered a man who would play a significant role in the next chapter of my story. Introduced through mutual friends, I found myself drawn to Mr. Charming's kindness, humor, and understanding nature. Our conversations flowed effortlessly, and I felt a connection that transcended the surface level.

In the days that followed the wedding, we continued to spend time together, exploring our shared interests and engaging in meaningful conversations. Mr.Charming's presence was a breath of fresh air, reminding me that meaningful connections were possible even after heartbreak. As we shared stories of our respective journeys, I found myself inspired by Mr.Charming's own path of growth and transformation.

While the timing of this new connection felt unexpected, my experiences had taught me to embrace the present moment. I approached my burgeoning relationship with Mr.Charming with an open heart and a sense of cautious optimism. We shared our values, our aspirations, and our commitment to personal growth—a foundation that held the potential for a deep and meaningful connection.

In the midst of this newfound connection, I remained mindful of my role as a parent. I made sure to communicate openly with Mr.Charming about my child and my responsibilities, ensuring that he understood the importance of my commitment to motherhood. Mr. Charming, in turn, showed genuine interest and respect for my role as a mom, recognizing that it is an integral part of who I am.

As our relationship developed, I also made a conscious effort to maintain the support system I had built throughout my journey. I remained connected to my therapist, my friends, and my community, seeking guidance and encouragement as I navigated this new chapter. My experiences had taught me the value of nurturing my own well-being, and I continued to prioritize self-care and growth.

My journey with Mr. Charming became a partnership built on mutual respect, shared values, and a deep understanding of each other's paths. We faced challenges together, supported one another's aspirations, and learned from each other's experiences. Mr.Charming's presence in my life is a testament to the possibility of finding love, connection, and growth even after facing significant adversity.

Writing My Heart's Desires

As I approached the completion of my master's degree, I continued to reflect on how far I had come. The journey had been demanding, and I had faced moments of doubt and exhaustion, but I had emerged stronger, wiser, and more empowered than ever. I delve into a transformation period where I devoted my days to fervently praying for my education, career goals, and my future husband, an act that set the stage for the growth and love story of a lifetime. As the ink flowed onto the crisp, white pages of my journal, so did my hopes, dreams, and desires. Each day, I took a few precious moments to craft silent prayers and a letter to God, outlining my goals I would like to achieve, along with the qualities and attributes I wished for in a life partner. It was a practice that grounded me. This gave me purpose, a daily ritual that would eventually lead me to my achievements and to the love of my life.

As my relationship with Mr.Charming began to blossom, I knew that I had to be proactive in building a strong foundation. I had learned the importance of having a support system during my earlier trials and tribulations, and I was determined to maintain it as I navigated this exciting new chapter.

My therapist, a steady guiding presence in my life, remained an integral part of my support network. She helped me navigate the complexities of a deepening relationship, offering insights and a safe space for me to express my fears and uncertainties. Through her guidance, I was able to develop the emotional tools necessary to nurture a loving partnership.

My friends, who had been with me since the inception of my quest for love, celebrated my newfound happiness with unwavering support. They provided advice, listened empathetically to my thoughts and concerns, and joined me in the jubilation of my growing love story. Our bond remained unbreakable, a testament to the power of enduring friendships.

Beyond my immediate circle, my community remained an essential part of my life. Engaging in volunteer work and activities that brought me joy was not just a way to give back but also a means to find purpose beyond my relationship.

Jamaica Dreams and a Proposal to Remember

Our trip to Jamaica had been a birthday getaway filled with laughter, adventure, and a deepening connection. The love between us had grown stronger with each passing day, and it was clear that we were building something beautiful together. Yet, I could sense something extraordinary was on the horizon.

One magical evening, as we strolled along the pristine, moonlit beach towards a candlelit dinner, hand in hand, I felt a flutter of excitement in the pit of my stomach. The sound of the waves crashing against the shore was the perfect soundtrack to our love story.

And then, under the canopy of stars that seemed to shine brighter just for us, Mr. Charming dropped to one knee. His voice trembled with emotion as he poured out his heart, professing his love and devotion. Tears welled up in both our eyes, mingling with the gentle lapping of the waves, as he asked the question that would change our lives forever.

In that tearful, heartfelt moment, I said yes, my voice filled with joy and gratitude. We held each other tightly, the weight of our dreams and the depth of our love filling the warm Jamaican night. It was a proposal that transcended words, a shared experience that etched itself into our hearts forever.

As my relationship with my future husband continued to evolve, I remained steadfast in my commitment to nurturing a strong foundation. Our shared journey had taught me the enduring value of a support system. I had learned that love was not just about two people; it was about the community that supported us, the friends who cheered us on, and the shared moments that made our love story truly unforgettable.

Jamaica had become the backdrop to a chapter in our love story that we would revisit time and time again. It was the place where our love had deepened, where we had cried tears of joy together, and where we had made promises that would last a lifetime. Our journey was far from over, but with each passing day, our foundation grew stronger, and our love deeper.

A Tapestry of Resilience

In the tapestry of life rich with lessons and inspirations, underscores the importance of nurturing a robust support system. Therapists, family, friends, and the embrace of a caring community played pivotal roles in this odyssey of transformation. Their unwavering presence, guidance, and encouragement provided a lifeline when the journey seemed treacherous.

A pivotal moment begins with crafting daily prayers, articulating desires and dreams for the future. These intentions became the driving force, guiding my steps towards a destiny that surpassed my most fervent hopes.

In the midst of my personal growth and self-discovery, love emerged as a cornerstone. My commitment to nurturing a strong foundation within my partnership serves as a profound reminder that love could be both a destination and a journey.

Amidst the lush beauty of Jamaica, an unforgettable proposal marked the apex of our love story. Tears of joy and gratitude flowed freely, encapsulating the profound growth and transformation that had occurred.

Central to this is the choice to heal. My courageous decision to confront my past and traumas, seek therapeutic guidance, and engage in self-care; I hope shines as a beacon of hope for others embarking on a similar path. Healing is not just a destination but an ongoing journey, a testament to true resilience and inner strength. As I close this chapter, I continue to pray for each chapter and season of my life moving forward. Continue to strive with a mustard seed of faith and watch God move mountains.

My Journal Notes

CHAPTER 5 THE WAKE-UP CALL
ALEXIS'S STORY

I remember it like it was yesterday. I was so excited because it was my favorite day of the week, FRIDAY! It was not just my favorite day but it was First Friday which meant Next Generation Youth and Young Adult Ministries were having our monthly YPFF (Youth Prophetic Flow Fridays). This particular night service was called the "Fill Up". I invited so many people & since I'm the assistant Youth leader and helped with the planning, I knew the lineup was going to be lit! That day I wore one of my best outfits that would compliment my new wig and you already know that it left me no other choice but to put my lashes on and come BIG! After work, I decided to pamper myself with getting my nails and eyebrows done so you already know I was feeling myself. I had such an amazing day at work and enjoyed treating myself that time crept up on me so fast. It was already 6pm and the service was set to start at 7:30pm which left me enough time to get some gas and pick up some people.

After getting gas, I was en route to pick up my crew and as I'm getting on the highway and passing the traffic light by the gas station, I could feel a force pushing my car & it felt as though it was coming through my back seat. While feeling the force from behind, I'm watching the front hood fold and bend causing my front windshield to crack all over.

All of this was happening because someone driving a U-Haul hit my car from behind and pushed my car into the left turning lane. The U-Haul literally was in my trunk which shoved me into the back of the car in front of me and in return, my car pushed that person into a truck that was making a left turn on the opposite side of us. All of this was within 10 minutes. I was in total shock! I immediately realize that I'm locked in my car and wondering if anything is broken. I look down to take my seatbelt off, my nose bleeding profusely, the smell of rubber & smoke was overwhelming and with urgency I'm trying to quickly get out of the car. Out of nowhere a man was at my car door trying to help get me out and make sure I'm okay. The man then walked me to the curve and that's when I called my mom; the ambulance and police were called and upon arrival, they were assessing the scene to see what happened. Everyone was shocked and kept asking "are you the one that was in the white car"?

The ONLY thing that was running through my mind was, 'if I wasn't taking my time getting my nails done and getting gas this wouldn't have happened'; 'Or if I hadn't changed from the middle lane to the left lane I wouldn't have gotten hit. After the "what if's", it was the "why me". It was like the devil was trying to take control of my thoughts and place me in a state of shock and fear. I was left without a car, all my work materials, dance apparel, and personal items were destroyed. Not to mention my nose was broken and I was left in pain and bruises. In the midst of that, very quickly and surely enough, my "why me and what ifs" turn into a "thank you Jesus".

After the accident and the emergency room I was adamant about still going to church and yes, I made it in time to praise Jesus that night.

That accident pushed me to live ON and IN PURPOSE. It taught me to not to be careless with my life but to go for everything like it's my last day on earth. It was a WAKE-UP CALL for me! It was a call to fully walk in my purpose and call, to stand and to go for broke! It caused a new fire to stir up within me and a new determination to BE all that God made me.

After the accident, moving forward hasn't been easy. Sometimes fear tries to show its ugly head but one thing I do know is that God hasn't given me that spirit at all. I have a spirit of Power, Love and a Sound Mind. I have to silence the voice of doubt and fear, not allowing it to have a space in my inner thoughts. From that situation, it has taught me who I AM. I know who I AM in life AND in the KINGDOM. So, I challenge you to know who you are & make every worst possible scenario, situation, even tragedy work to your advantage. Yes, it hurt but it was for your good. This is what Romans 8:28 has taught me; It will all be worth it because God can and will use it for your good.

That Monday after the accident which was about 3 days later, I was starting my student teaching job. My principal at the time was very concerned and wanted me to stay out a semester due to the severity of the accident, but you already know that I declared and decreed that I would graduate on time which meant I would complete my student teaching during the time expected and no delays! Glad to say I did! I couldn't be stopped…why? I knew my authority. Do you know yours?

Sometimes the enemy wants to make you or have people block blessings and promotions or label you from your past/tragedy. That wasn't going to be so for me and it will not be so for you either. I came out of my accident walking, in my right mind and I recovered from surgery within 3 days. If it was decided by man, I should've been dead that day but I'm alive. That means nobody or nothing is going to hold me down.

Sister…..brother, I say unto you no it won't be easy; it may not go your way but you got this. This is your sign; this is your confirmation to take the baton and run. THIS IS YOUR WAKE-UP CALL. Take heed to the clarion call.

My Journal Notes

We hope and pray this book leads all who have read it to make an active choice and HEAL so you can become a BETTER VERSION of yourself.

There's More To Come!

I CHOOSE TO HEAL!

Made in the USA
Middletown, DE
23 July 2024